TOILETRIVIA ™

HOCKEY

The only trivia book that caters to your everyday bathroom needs

by Jeremy Klaff & Harry Klaff

This book might contain product names, trademarks, or registered trade-marks. All trademarks in this book are property of their respective owners. If used, they are for non-biased use, and we do not encourage or discourage use of said product or service. Any term suspected of being a trademark will be properly capitalized.

Cover art by Stephanie Strack

©2012 Toiletrivia by Jeremy Klaff and Harry Klaff. Reproduction in whole or in part without written permission of the publisher is strictly prohibited.

About the Authors

Harry Klaff covered the NHL for *The Hockey News* and *Hockey Pictorial*, and reported for both the Associated Press and United Press International. He has written three books, *All Time Greatest Super Bowl*, *All Time Greatest Stanley Cup*, and *Computer Literacy and Use*.

Today, he is a retired Social Studies teacher from Brooklyn. Because he never went on a date in his adolescence, Harry had plenty of time to research useless facts and figures on everything ranging from history to pop culture. Moonlighting as a hockey scoreboard operator and baseball beer vendor, Harry had ample time to collect data.

Yet somehow, he got married. In 1977, Jeremy was born. Rather than being raised on a steady diet of carrots and peas, baby Jeremy was forced to learn facts from textbooks. His first word was "Uzbekistan." Throughout his childhood, Jeremy had a hard time making friends. When other kids wanted to play baseball, he wanted to instruct them about Henry VIII's six wives. After a failed career as a standup comic and broadcaster, in 2000 Jeremy fittingly became a Social Studies teacher. Today he brings trivia to the next generation.

Collect All Toiletrivia Titles

US History

World History

Pop Culture

Sports

Baseball

Music

and more!

Get the full list of titles at
www.toiletrivia.com

Acknowledgements

We at Toiletrivia would like to thank all of the people who made this possible.

- •The ancient cities of Harappa and Mohenjo Daro for engineering advances in plumbing.

- •Sir John Harrington for inventing the modern flush toilet.

- •Seth Wheeler for his patent of perforated toilet paper.

- •Jeffrey Gunderson for inventing the plunger.

We would like to thank our families for suffering through nights of endless trivia.

We would also like to thank the friendly commuters at the Grand Central Station restroom facility for field testing these editions.

Introduction

Here at *Toiletrivia* we do extensive research on what you, the bathroom user, wish to see in your reading material. Sure, there are plenty of fine books out there to pass the time, but none of them cater to your competitive needs. That's why *Toiletrivia* is here to provide captivating trivia that allows you to interact with fellow bathroom users.

Each chapter allows you to keep score so you can evaluate your progress if you choose to go through the book multiple times. Or, you may wish to leave the book behind for others to play and keep score against you. Perhaps you just want to make it look like you are a genius, and leave a perfect scorecard for all to see. We hope you leave one in every bathroom of the house.

The rules of *Toiletrivia* are simple. Each chapter has 30 questions divided into three sections…One Roll, Two Rolls, or Three Rolls. The One Rolls are easiest and worth one point. Two Rolls are a bit harder and are worth two points. And of course, Three Rolls are the hardest, and are worth three points. You will tabulate your progress on the scorecard near the end of the book.

The questions we have selected are meant for dinner conversation, or impressing people you want to date. With few exceptions, our queries are geared for the uncomfortable situations that life throws at you, like when you have nothing in common with someone, and need to offer some clever banter. We hope that the facts you learn in the restroom make it easier to meet your future in-laws, or deal with that hairdresser who just won't stop talking to you.

Remember, *Toiletrivia* is a game. No joysticks, no computer keyboards…just you, your toilet, and a pen; the way nature intended it. So good luck. We hope you are triumphant.

DIRECTIONS

Each set of questions has an answer sheet opposite it. Write your answers in the first available column to the right. When you are done with a set of 10 questions, *fold* your answer column underneath so the next restroom user doesn't see your answers. *Special note to restroom users 2 and 3: No cheating! And the previous person's answers might be wrong!*

Then check your responses with the answer key in the back of the book. Mark your right answers with a check, and your wrong answers with an "x." Then go to the scorecard on pages 98-100 and tabulate your results. These totals will be the standard for other users to compare.

Be sure to look online for other Toiletrivia titles
Visit us at www.toiletrivia.com

Table of Contents

Greatest Moments

Flip to pg. 68 for answers

 ## One Roll

1. What was Al Michaels referring to on February 22, 1980 when he asked, "Do you believe in miracles?"

2. Who scored the winning goal in overtime on March 10, 2010 to give Canada the Olympic gold medal over the US?

3. On March 12, 1966, he became the first player to score more than 50 goals in a season. Who is he?

4. On June 9, 2010, whose Game 6 OT goal gave the Blackhawks their first Stanley Cup since 1961?

5. The struggling Pittsburgh Penguins franchise got a breath of optimism on June 9, 1984, when they chose him with the number one pick in the NHL Entry Draft.

6. On March 28, 1982, he scored his record 92nd goal of the season.

7. On May 24, 1980, whose OT goal gave the New York Islanders their first Stanley Cup?

8. On March 17, 2009, Martin Brodeur won his 552nd game. Who did he pass as the all-time leader in wins?

9. On November 1, 1959, Jacques Plante changed goaltending forever. What did he do?

10. On October 15, 1989, Wayne Gretzky tied and then passed Gordie Howe as the NHL's all-time leading scorer. What city was the fateful backdrop to the record?

Answer Sheet | Answer Sheet | Answer Sheet

Greatest Moments 1 Roll	Greatest Moments 1 Roll	Greatest Moments 1 Roll
Name_____	Name_____	Name_____
1.	1.	1.
2.	2.	2.
3.	3.	3.
4.	4.	4.
5.	5.	5.
6.	6.	6.
7.	7.	7.
8.	8.	8.
9.	9.	9.
10.	10.	10.

After you have filled out the sheet, fold your column underneath along the dashed line so the next restroom user won't see your answers. *The first player uses the far right column.*

Notes: | *Notes:* | *Notes:*

Greatest Moments

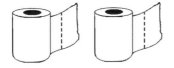

Two Rolls

Flip to pg. 69 for answers

1. Who was knocked unconscious in Game 7 of the Stanley Cup semifinals on April 8, 1952, but returned late in the game to score the winning goal?

2. What record did Toronto's Darryl Sittler set on February 7, 1976?

3. On October 9, 2010, this Ranger became the most recent player to record a hat trick in his first NHL game.

4. This man became the first player of African descent to play in the NHL on January 18, 1958. Who was he?

5. What happened at Squaw Valley, California on February 28, 1960?

6. On March 21, 1985, he became the first US-born player to score 50 goals in a season.

7. "Matteau! Matteau! Matteau!," screamed broadcaster Howie Rose on May 27, 1994. What happened?

8. On April 19, 1987, whose fourth-OT goal lifted the Islanders to victory in Game 7 against the Capitals? He scored at about 2 a.m. Easter morning.

9. What happened on September 2, 1972 that Canadian newspapers proclaimed, "A National Disaster"?

10. The NHL established a midseason precedent on February 14, 1934. What was it?

Answer Sheet

Greatest Moments
2 Rolls

Name_____

1.
2.
3.
4.
5.
6.
7.
8.
9.
10.

Answer Sheet

Greatest Moments
2 Rolls

Name_____

1.
2.
3.
4.
5.
6.
7.
8.
9.
10.

Answer Sheet

Greatest Moments
2 Rolls

Name_____

1.
2.
3.
4.
5.
6.
7.
8.
9.
10.

After you have filled out the sheet, fold your column underneath along the dashed line so the next restroom user won't see your answers. ***The first player uses the far right column.***

Notes: *Notes:*   *Notes:*

Greatest Moments

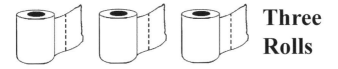

Three Rolls

Flip to pg. 70 for answers

1. What did Detroit's Mud Bruneteau accomplish on March 24, 1936? It's surprising that he was even awake to celebrate.

2. This Toronto defenseman's OT goal against the Canadiens won the Stanley Cup for Toronto in 1951. Tragically, he died in a small plane crash four months later.

3. What did Calgary's Theoren Fleury do on March 9, 1991 which made the St. Louis Blues cringe every time they went on a power play?

4. On January 31, 1920, Joe Malone of the Quebec Bulldogs set a record that still stands. What is it?

5. Within 5 seconds, how long did it take Chicago's Bill Mosienko to score three goals on March 23, 1952?

6. On November 7, 1968, he became the only visiting team player to score 6 goals in a game.

7. On March 3, 1920, the Montreal Canadiens set a record for most goals in one game. Within one, how many did they score?

8. On February 28, 1929, the Chicago Blackhawks set an ignominious record, as they were shut out yet again. How many games in a row were they held off the scoreboard?

9. On February 2, 1977, this Leaf set a defenseman's record by scoring 5 goals in one game.

10. His Game 7 double-OT goal on April 23, 1950 won the Stanley Cup for the Detroit Red Wings.

Answer Sheet

Greatest Moments
3 Rolls

Name_____

Answer Sheet

Greatest Moments
3 Rolls

Name_____

Answer Sheet

Greatest Moments
3 Rolls

Name_____

1.	1.	1.
2.	2.	2.
3.	3.	3.
4.	4.	4.
5.	5.	5.
6.	6.	6.
7.	7.	7.
8.	8.	8.
9.	9.	9.
10.	10.	10.

After you have filled out the sheet, fold your column underneath along the dashed line so the next restroom user won't see your answers. ***The first player uses the far right column.***

Notes: *Notes:*   *Notes:*

13

Wings & Centers

 One Roll

Flip to pg. 71 for answers

1. This Chicago Blackhawk great was known as "The Golden Jet."

2. What New York Islanders sniper scored 53 goals in his first season and went on to score 50 or more 9 consecutive times?

3. This Philadelphia Flyers left winger holds the record for most penalty minutes in a season with 472.

4. In 1970-71, who scored 76 goals and 76 assists to set a single-season scoring record? This record has been shattered many times since.

5. This scrappy little center holds many Los Angeles Kings scoring records.

6. Name all four NHL teams that Wayne Gretzky played for.

7. As of the end of the 2011-12 season, who had the most career assists by an active player?

8. Which US-born player has the most career goals?

9. Which Calgary Flame scored his 500th goal, 1,000th point, and hoisted the Stanley Cup in his final NHL season? He had one of the best mustaches in the league…but in 1989 he added a rugged playoff beard.

10. Alex Ovechkin was taken number one overall by the Capitals in the 2004 NHL Entry Draft. The Penguins took another USSR-born player as number two. Who is he?

Answer Sheet

Wings & Centers
1 Roll

Name_____

Answer Sheet

Wings & Centers
1 Roll

Name_____

Answer Sheet

Wings & Centers
1 Roll

Name_____

1.	1.	1.
2.	2.	2.
3.	3.	3.
4.	4.	4.
5.	5.	5.
6.	6.	6.
7.	7.	7.
8.	8.	8.
9.	9.	9.
10.	10.	10.

After you have filled out the sheet, fold your column underneath along the dashed line so the next restroom user won't see your answers. ***The first player uses the far right column.***

Notes:

Notes:

Notes:

Wings & Centers

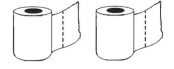

Two Rolls

Flip to pg. 72 for answers

1. This right winger, who learned the game playing roller hockey in the streets on the West Side of Manhattan, notched 502 career goals. Name him.

2. What left winger had his #9 retired by the New York Islanders? He was also one of the best fighters of the 1980s.

3. Left winger Dave (Tiger) Williams holds a record that not too many would be proud of. What is it?

4. Name the Toronto left winger who scored 48 goals in 1960-61.

5. This long-time Hartford Whaler finished his career second only to Wayne Gretzky in all-time assists. He ended the 1995-96 season tied with his Penguin teammate, Mario Lemieux, with 92 assists to lead the league. Name him.

6. Who holds the record for most career goals by a left winger? He played mostly for the Los Angeles Kings.

7. Known as "The Roadrunner," this right wing scored 428 career goals for the Montreal Canadiens.

8. Any goal-scorer would want this guy feeding him the puck. He led the league in assists three times, setting up goals for Brett Hull in St. Louis, Cam Neely in Boston, and Peter Bondra in Washington.

9. In 1992-93, this Winnipeg Jet set a record for most goals in a season by a rookie with 76. Who is he?

10. Among all-time goal scorers, Wayne Gretzky is tops with 894. Gordie Howe is second with 801. Who is third with 741?

Answer Sheet

Wings & Centers
2 Rolls

Name_____

1.
2.
3.
4.
5.
6.
7.
8.
9.
10.

Answer Sheet

Wings & Centers
2 Rolls

Name_____

1.
2.
3.
4.
5.
6.
7.
8.
9.
10.

Answer Sheet

Wings & Centers
2 Rolls

Name_____

1.
2.
3.
4.
5.
6.
7.
8.
9.
10.

After you have filled out the sheet, fold your column underneath along the dashed line so the next restroom user won't see your answers. *The first player uses the far right column.*

Notes:

Notes:

Notes:

Wings & Centers

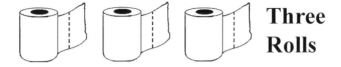

Three Rolls

Flip to pg. 73 for answers

1. Name one of the two teams that Gordie Howe played for in the WHA.

2. Who was the great superstar of the 1930s, whose #7 was retired by the Montreal Canadiens shortly after he died on March 8, 1937?

3. The New York Rangers GAG Line was so named because it seemed they scored a Goal A Game. Name two of its members.

4. Who was the WHA's all-time leading scorer?

5. No one ever scored 1,000 points in a Winnipeg Jets uniform. What center came pretty close?

6. What was the name of the famed Detroit Red Wings line of Gordie Howe, Sid Abel, and Ted Lindsay?

7. His #19 was retired by the Minnesota North Stars after he died following an on-ice accident on January 15, 1968. Today an NHL trophy is named for him.

8. The 1983 NHL Entry Draft featured future stars such as Pat LaFontaine, Steve Yzerman, and Dominik Hasek (who was taken in the 10th round). Who did the Minnesota North Stars take with the first overall pick?

9. A center for Montreal, Washington, and Hartford holds the record for playing in the most consecutive games. Who is he?

10. The Bruins had a famous line of German-Canadians in the 1940s consisting of Milt Schmidt, Bobby Bauer, and Woody Dumart. What was it nicknamed?

Answer Sheet Answer Sheet Answer Sheet

Wings & Centers
3 Rolls

Wings & Centers
3 Rolls

Wings & Centers
3 Rolls

Name_____ Name_____ Name_____

1.	1.	1.
2.	2.	2.
3.	3.	3.
4.	4.	4.
5.	5.	5.
6.	6.	6.
7.	7.	7.
8.	8.	8.
9.	9.	9.
10.	10.	10.

After you have filled out the sheet, fold your column underneath along the dashed line so the next restroom user won't see your answers. *The first player uses the far right column.*

Notes: *Notes:*   *Notes:*

Between the Pipes

 ## One Roll

Flip to pg. 74 for answers

1. Good luck spelling this guy's last name in Scrabble, as it contains every vowel in the alphabet. Notably, he brought the young Florida Panthers organization to the Stanley Cup Finals in 1996. Name him.

2. This Swede was the steal of the 2000 NHL Entry Draft, as the New York Rangers took him 205th overall. By 2006, he was "King" of the Olympics, leading Sweden to their second-ever gold medal.

3. What record-breaking goalie was chosen behind Craig Billington and Daryl Reaught in the 1984 NHL Entry Draft? He retired in 2003 as the winningest goaltender in NHL history.

4. The trophy given to the NHL's best goaltender is called the Vezina Trophy. Who was Vezina?

5. Who has the most career penalty minutes by a goaltender?

6. What Vancouver netminder helped Canada win the gold medal at the 2010 Winter Olympic Games?

7. This Cornell product led the Montreal Canadiens to six Stanley Cups.

8. Just because this goalie never won the Stanley Cup doesn't mean his career "went to the dogs." He finished his career with 454 wins.

9. Who is the only New York Islander to win the Vezina Trophy? He was known to whack an ankle or two if you invaded his goal crease.

10. If it wasn't for Jim Carey of the Washington Capitals in 1996, this Buffalo Sabre goalie would have won the Vezina Trophy from 1994-1999. He added one more in 2001 for good measure.

Answer Sheet

Between the Pipes
1 Roll

Name_____

Answer Sheet

Between the Pipes
1 Roll

Name_____

Answer Sheet

Between the Pipes
1 Roll

Name_____

1.	1.	1.
2.	2.	2.
3.	3.	3.
4.	4.	4.
5.	5.	5.
6.	6.	6.
7.	7.	7.
8.	8.	8.
9.	9.	9.
10.	10.	10.

After you have filled out the sheet, fold your column underneath along the dashed line so the next restroom user won't see your answers. *The first player uses the far right column.*

Notes: *Notes:*   *Notes:*

Between the Pipes

Two Rolls

Flip to pg. 75 for answers

1. Glenn Hall holds a goaltending record that will probably never be broken. What is it?

2. Who was the first goaltender to score a goal in the modern era?

3. On March 4, 1941, Chicago's Sam LoPresti faced the most shots ever in a regular season NHL game. Within 5, how many shots did Boston fire at him?

4. What Latvian netminder led the Carolina Hurricanes to their first Stanley Cup Final in 2002?

5. The Rangers had a terrible, bow-legged goalie during WWII named Steve Buzinski. A Toronto paper had a rhyming caption of him, "This is Steve Buzinski, he lets the pucks go_____."

6. Until the mid-1960s, teams only carried one goaltender. If he was injured and couldn't continue, what happened?

7. This former Detroit Red Wing goalie returned to Detroit to back up Dominik Hasek in 2007. He did so well, that he gained the starting job, and led his team to a Stanley Cup months later. Name him.

8. What Finnish Flame recorded the lowest GAA in the modern era with a 1.69 in 2003-2004? He helped the Flames reach the Stanley Cup Finals.

9. George Hainsworth of the Montreal Canadiens holds the all-time record for most shutouts in a season with 22. But who has the post-1930 mark with 15? He did it in 1969-70.

10. This goaltender painted "stitches" on his mask to show what would have happened to his face if he wasn't wearing it.

Answer Sheet

Between the Pipes
2 Rolls

Name_____

1.
2.
3.
4.
5.
6.
7.
8.
9.
10.

Answer Sheet

Between the Pipes
2 Rolls

Name_____

1.
2.
3.
4.
5.
6.
7.
8.
9.
10.

Answer Sheet

Between the Pipes
2 Rolls

Name_____

1.
2.
3.
4.
5.
6.
7.
8.
9.
10.

After you have filled out the sheet, fold your column underneath along the dashed line so the next restroom user won't see your answers. ***The first player uses the far right column.***

Notes: *Notes:*   *Notes:*

Between the Pipes

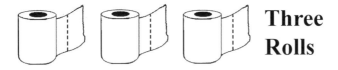

Three Rolls

Flip to pg. 76 for answers

1. This Toronto netminder led the Leafs to consecutive Stanley Cup victories in 1962, 1963, and 1964. In 1969, he became the oldest goaltender (age 44) to play in a Stanley Cup playoff game.

2. It was one of the most gruesome injuries in hockey history. What Buffalo goalie was slashed in the jugular by the skate of Steve Tuttle in 1989?

3. The star goaltender of the 1960 US Olympic team played a few games for the Rangers before settling on a career in the minors. Name him.

4. This American-born Bruins goalie of the 1930s and 40s was known as "Mr. Zero."

5. From 2000-2003, two goalies were taken first overall in the NHL Entry Draft. Who are they?

6. The longest winning streak by a goaltender is held by a Boston Bruin. Name him.

7. This pair of Rangers shared the Vezina Trophy in 1970-71, marking the first time a Blueshirt had won the hardware since Davey Kerr did it in 1939-40.

8. As late as the 1960s, what did most goaltenders use for a catching glove?

9. Gary Smith of the California Golden Seals holds a record he wishes he didn't have. What's the record?

10. Whose career shutout record did Martin Brodeur break when he notched his 104th whitewash on December 21, 2009?

Answer Sheet   Answer Sheet   Answer Sheet

Between the Pipes
3 Rolls

Between the Pipes
3 Rolls

Between the Pipes
3 Rolls

Name_____   Name_____   Name_____

1.	1.	1.
2.	2.	2.
3.	3.	3.
4.	4.	4.
5.	5.	5.
6.	6.	6.
7.	7.	7.
8.	8.	8.
9.	9.	9.
10.	10.	10.

After you have filled out the sheet, fold your column underneath along the dashed line so the next restroom user won't see your answers. ***The first player uses the far right column.***

Notes: *Notes:*   *Notes:*

Stanley Cup Playoffs

 One Roll

Flip to pg. 77 for answers

1. What team has won the most Stanley Cups?

2. Why wasn't the Stanley Cup awarded in 2005?

3. Entering the 2012 playoffs, two goaltenders shared the record for most career Cup shutouts. Name one of these two goalies.

4. What player has played for the most Stanley Cup champions?

5. Who was the first post-1967 expansion team to win the Stanley Cup?

6. What is the 16th Earl of Derby more commonly known as?

7. Within two seconds, what was the shortest overtime in Stanley Cup history?

8. Who has scored the most career playoff goals?

9. Who has coached the most Stanley Cup champions?

10. Colorado's Joe Sakic has a record eight of these.

Answer Sheet   Answer Sheet   Answer Sheet

Stanley Cup Playoffs
1 Roll

Stanley Cup Playoffs
1 Roll

Stanley Cup Playoffs
1 Roll

Name_____   Name_____   Name_____

1.	1.	1.
2.	2.	2.
3.	3.	3.
4.	4.	4.
5.	5.	5.
6.	6.	6.
7.	7.	7.
8.	8.	8.
9.	9.	9.
10.	10.	10.

After you have filled out the sheet, fold your column underneath along the dashed line so the next restroom user won't see your answers. ***The first player uses the far right column.***

Notes: *Notes:*   *Notes:*

Stanley Cup Playoffs

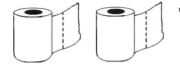

Two Rolls

Flip to pg. 78 for answers

1. Who is the only person to win the Conn Smythe Trophy (playoff MVP) *before* he won the Calder Trophy (league's best rookie) the following year?

2. Only three teams have come back from a 3-0 deficit in playoff history (1942, 1975, and 2010). Name two of these teams.

3. He has the most playoff penalty minutes in league history with 729. However, his most infamous penalty was when he blindsided Islander Pierre Turgeon in Game 6 of the 1993 Division Semifinals.

4. A US-born defenseman holds the record for making the playoffs the most times. Who is he?

5. Which team holds the record for appearing in the Stanley Cup playoffs for the most consecutive years?

6. Many fans do not realize that the Stanley Cup they see presented every spring is not the original. Where is the original located?

7. Three teams from places that would have been in the Confederate States of America during the Civil War have won the Stanley Cup. Name two of them.

8. He won eight Stanley Cups as a player, and then coached a Stanley Cup champion in 1995.

9. What US-based team has won the most Stanley Cups?

10. As we've noted, the most valuable player in the Stanley Cup playoffs receives the Conn Smythe Trophy. Who was Conn Smythe?

Answer Sheet

Stanley Cup Playoffs
2 Rolls

Name_____

Answer Sheet

Stanley Cup Playoffs
2 Rolls

Name_____

Answer Sheet

Stanley Cup Playoffs
2 Rolls

Name_____

1.	1.	1.
2.	2.	2.
3.	3.	3.
4.	4.	4.
5.	5.	5.
6.	6.	6.
7.	7.	7.
8.	8.	8.
9.	9.	9.
10.	10.	10.

After you have filled out the sheet, fold your column underneath along the dashed line so the next restroom user won't see your answers. *The first player uses the far right column.*

Notes:

Notes:

Notes:

Stanley Cup Playoffs

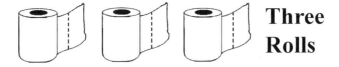

Three Rolls

Flip to pg. 79 for answers

1. It was quite the upset in 1993 when this Prague-born New York Islander beat Tom Barrasso in OT to send the heavily favored Penguins packing.

2. Who was the first US-based team to win the Stanley Cup? We'll give you a hint. That city's Totems were in the Western Hockey League in the 1950s-70s, and are currently in the Northern Pacific (Jr.) Hockey League.

3. In Game 6 of the 1964 Finals against Detroit, this Toronto defenseman broke his leg, but returned in overtime to score the winning goal.

4. In a matter of months in 1938, he coached the Chicago Blackhawks to a Stanley Cup, and umpired Johnny Vander Meer's second consecutive no-hitter. He is also the *only* person to coach a Stanley Cup winner and umpire a World Series game. Name him.

5. Every so often until 1914, the Stanley Cup was not awarded to the team who won the most games in the finals. How was the winner determined?

6. Two Americans have captained a Stanley Cup champion. Name one.

7. In 1905, One-Eyed Frank McGee of the Ottawa Silver Seven set a record for most goals in a Stanley Cup Finals game. Within 2, how many did he score?

8. What does a team called the Montreal AAA (not the auto club) have to do with Stanley Cup history?

9. Why wasn't the Stanley Cup awarded in 1919?

10. What team has won the most consecutive playoff series?

Answer Sheet

Stanley Cup Playoffs
3 Rolls

Name_____

Answer Sheet

Stanley Cup Playoffs
3 Rolls

Name_____

Answer Sheet

Stanley Cup Playoffs
3 Rolls

Name_____

1.	1.	1.
2.	2.	2.
3.	3.	3.
4.	4.	4.
5.	5.	5.
6.	6.	6.
7.	7.	7.
8.	8.	8.
9.	9.	9.
10.	10.	10.

After you have filled out the sheet, fold your column underneath along the dashed line so the next restroom user won't see your answers. *The first player uses the far right column.*

Notes: *Notes:*   *Notes:*

Defensemen

One Roll

Flip to pg. 80 for answers

1. What long-time Bruin finally won the Stanley Cup as a member of the 2001 Colorado Avalanche?

2. The first pick in the 1973 NHL Amateur Draft, he later captained the New York Islanders to their four Stanley Cups.

3. Back in the "old days," you could usually tell that a player was a defenseman by looking at his uniform number. How?

4. He won the Norris Memorial Trophy as the league's best defenseman in 2004 for New Jersey, and the Conn Smythe Trophy for Anaheim in 2007.

5. First he was a US Olympian, and then he played from 1983-2010 with Montreal, Chicago, Detroit, and Atlanta. He appeared in 1,651 games, the most by any defenseman in NHL history. Name him.

6. This defenseman was the first American-born winner of the Conn Smythe Trophy.

7. The son of two Jamaican immigrants, in 2011 he became the first Montreal defenseman to record a hat trick in his rookie season.

8. Who was the first European-born defenseman to win the Norris Trophy?

9. Ottawa captain Daniel Alfredsson was thrilled with the Senators' top pick in the 2008 NHL Entry Draft. That's because it was this fellow Swede who would become the 2012 Norris Trophy winner. Who is he?

10. This Edmonton Oiler scored the most goals by a defenseman in a season - 48.

Answer Sheet | Answer Sheet | Answer Sheet

Defensemen
1 Roll

Name_____

Defensemen 1 Roll	Defensemen 1 Roll	Defensemen 1 Roll
1.	1.	1.
2.	2.	2.
3.	3.	3.
4.	4.	4.
5.	5.	5.
6.	6.	6.
7.	7.	7.
8.	8.	8.
9.	9.	9.
10.	10.	10.

After you have filled out the sheet, fold your column underneath along the dashed line so the next restroom user won't see your answers. ***The first player uses the far right column.***

Notes: *Notes:*   *Notes:*

Defensemen

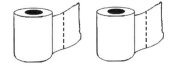

Two Rolls

Flip to pg. 81 for answers

1. This rugged D-man was nicknamed "Mr. Devil" among New Jersey fans, as #3 played every game of his career with them. Name him.

2. In 1980, he became the first player to win an Olympic hockey gold medal and the Stanley Cup in the same year.

3. Chosen first overall by the Florida Panthers in the 1994 NHL Entry Draft, he later played for Vancouver and Phoenix before returning to the Panthers in 2011-12.

4. He won six Stanley Cups with the Montreal Canadiens, and ended his career in 1968-69 with the St. Louis Blues at age 45.

5. This Hall of Fame Bruins defenseman of the 1920s and 30s later became the owner of the Springfield Indians of the AHL. He treated his players so poorly that they went on strike.

6. If it wasn't for the presence of one Robert Gordon Orr, this Ranger and Bruin might have been regarded as the greatest defensemen of the era. He finished second in the Norris Trophy balloting six times.

7. This Hall-of-Famer was an offensive force for the Washington Capitals from 1984-1994. He scored 34 goals in 1992-93.

8. Only one LA King has ever won the Norris Trophy. Who is he?

9. This bespectacled defenseman played on four Stanley Cup winners, then coached the New York Islanders to four more.

10. Who did the Hartford Whalers select with the second overall pick in the 1993 NHL Entry Draft? He later won the Hart Trophy with the Blues.

Answer Sheet | Answer Sheet | Answer Sheet

Defensemen
2 Rolls

Name_____

Defensemen
2 Rolls

Name_____

Defensemen
2 Rolls

Name_____

1.	1.	1.
2.	2.	2.
3.	3.	3.
4.	4.	4.
5.	5.	5.
6.	6.	6.
7.	7.	7.
8.	8.	8.
9.	9.	9.
10.	10.	10.

After you have filled out the sheet, fold your column underneath along the dashed line so the next restroom user won't see your answers. ***The first player uses the far right column.***

Notes: | *Notes:* | *Notes:*

Defensemen

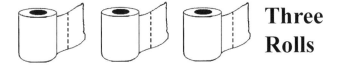

Three Rolls

Flip to pg. 82 for answers

1. One of the first Finnish defensemen in the NHL, he played seven seasons for the Rangers, Oilers, and Devils between 1981 and 1990. Spelling doesn't count.

2. The first Norris Trophy in 1954 was won by a Detroit player, who later became a center for Toronto and a member of Parliament.

3. One of the few Jewish players of the 1950s and 60s, "The Rock" played a few seasons for the Red Wings and Blackhawks, then resurfaced with the Philadelphia Flyers from 1967-69 after 12 years in the minors.

4. Originally a Montreal Canadien, he won successive Norris Trophies for the Washington Capitals in 1983 and 1984.

5. Traded by Toronto to Pittsburgh in 1978, he became the Penguins' only Norris Trophy winner in 1981.

6. He won the Calder Trophy in 1964, played on six Montreal Stanley Cup champions, and won two more Cups as an assistant coach for the Habs.

7. In Game 7 of the Division Finals, what Edmonton rookie defenseman put the puck in his own net on April 30, 1986? The goal decided the series.

8. This gentleman Rangers defenseman was fortunate to have his best year in 1966-67. He won the Norris Trophy that year just before Bobby Orr began his run of 8 trophies in a row.

9. The last Islander to win the Calder Trophy, he played for 6 teams in 10 years despite a serious eye injury.

10. This former captain of the Chicago Blackhawks won the Norris Trophy three years in a row from 1963-65.

Answer Sheet | Answer Sheet | Answer Sheet

Defensemen
3 Rolls

Defensemen
3 Rolls

Defensemen
3 Rolls

Name_____ Name_____ Name_____

1.	1.	1.
2.	2.	2.
3.	3.	3.
4.	4.	4.
5.	5.	5.
6.	6.	6.
7.	7.	7.
8.	8.	8.
9.	9.	9.
10.	10.	10.

After you have filled out the sheet, fold your column underneath along the dashed line so the next restroom user won't see your answers. *The first player uses the far right column.*

Notes: | *Notes:* | *Notes:*

Rules & Refs

 ## One Roll

Flip to pg. 83 for answers

1. What are the dimensions of a hockey net?

2. How many minutes is a major penalty?

3. Prior to 1983, what happened if a game ended in a tie after three periods?

4. "The puck hit the glass!" would be the only argument a player could have for what minor penalty?

5. What is the infraction called when an offensive player crosses the blue line before the puck?

6. Video reviews have made this once crucial off-ice official obsolete.

7. Within one-half of an inch, what is the diameter of a hockey puck?

8. What is the infraction called when a player shoots the puck from their half of the red line, across the opponent's goal line, and it is first touched by the opposition?

9. Which on-ice officials have the job of breaking up fights?

10. Within 2 inches, how wide are the blue lines?

Answer Sheet

Rules & Refs
1 Roll

Name_____

Answer Sheet

Rules & Refs
1 Roll

Name_____

Answer Sheet

Rules & Refs
1 Roll

Name_____

1.	1.	1.
2.	2.	2.
3.	3.	3.
4.	4.	4.
5.	5.	5.
6.	6.	6.
7.	7.	7.
8.	8.	8.
9.	9.	9.
10.	10.	10.

After you have filled out the sheet, fold your column underneath along the dashed line so the next restroom user won't see your answers. ***The first player uses the far right column.***

Notes:

Notes:

Notes:

Rules & Refs

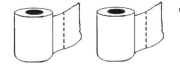

Two Rolls

Flip to pg. 84 for answers

1. What minor penalty was added in 1992 to prevent "bad acting" from players trying to draw a penalty?

2. No, he didn't walk on the moon, but he did serve as a linesman in over 1,700 NHL games.

3. What color armband do NHL referees wear to distinguish them from linesmen?

4. What is the signal for slashing?

5. Before 1991, what was the shape of the goal crease?

6. What is the call if a player makes contact with an opponent who is not in possession, or has not yet touched the puck?

7. A defending player, other than the goaltender, falls on the puck in the goal crease. What is the call?

8. What object serves as the guide for how high a stick can be when batting a puck into the goal?

9. What is the trapezoid marking behind the net for?

10. Snipers such as Bobby Hull and Stan Mikita hated a new rule that went into effect in 1967 regarding their hockey sticks. What was the rule?

Answer Sheet

Rules & Refs
2 Rolls

Name_____

Answer Sheet

Rules & Refs
2 Rolls

Name_____

Answer Sheet

Rules & Refs
2 Rolls

Name_____

1.	1.	1.
2.	2.	2.
3.	3.	3.
4.	4.	4.
5.	5.	5.
6.	6.	6.
7.	7.	7.
8.	8.	8.
9.	9.	9.
10.	10.	10.

After you have filled out the sheet, fold your column underneath along the dashed line so the next restroom user won't see your answers. *The first player uses the far right column.*

Notes: *Notes:* *Notes:*

Rules & Refs

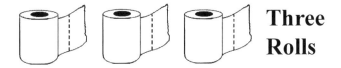

Three Rolls

Flip to pg. 85 for answers

1. In the mid-1900s, how was it determined what number a particular referee wore?

2. Known as "The Big Whistle," this New York-raised Hall-of-Fame referee served many years as a color commentator for the New York Rangers.

3. What is the call if a player deliberately kicks the puck with his skate to a teammate, who then knocks the puck into the net with his stick?

4. Within two years, when did the NHL eliminate the red line for two-line passes?

5. Who holds the record for refereeing the most NHL games?

6. A new rule that went into effect in 1956-57 aimed to lessen the impact of the Montreal Canadiens' devastating power play. What was this new rule?

7. What penalty is a referee calling when he rotates his fists in front of his body, similar to a football referee signaling a false start.

8. What is the signal for a penalty shot?

9. Why are the blue lines solid, but the red line is either checked or has a design running through it?

10. Within six inches, how wide is today's goal crease?

Answer Sheet

Rules & Refs
3 Rolls

Name_____

Answer Sheet

Rules & Refs
3 Rolls

Name_____

Answer Sheet

Rules & Refs
3 Rolls

Name_____

1.	1.	1.
2.	2.	2.
3.	3.	3.
4.	4.	4.
5.	5.	5.
6.	6.	6.
7.	7.	7.
8.	8.	8.
9.	9.	9.
10.	10.	10.

After you have filled out the sheet, fold your column underneath along the dashed line so the next restroom user won't see your answers. ***The first player uses the far right column.***

Notes:

Notes:

Notes:

The Original Six

 ## One Roll

Flip to pg. 86 for answers

1. Before expansion, there were "The Original Six" teams. Name all six.

2. Which team finished in first place seven straight years from 1948-49 through 1954-55?

3. What 18 year-old from Parry Sound, Ontario made his debut on October 19, 1966?

4. They were the Canadiens' "Rocket" and "Pocket Rocket."

5. A journeyman goaltender in his playing days, "The Cat" became coach of the Rangers in 1965. He later became the team's GM.

6. What night was *Hockey Night in Canada*?

7. This Montreal great was nicknamed "Boom Boom" because of the sound his slap shot made against the boards.

8. He was President of the NHL from 1946 until 1977.

9. He coached the Montreal Canadiens to eight Stanley Cups in 13 years in the 1950s and 1960s.

10. In the 1960s, it seems that one of the best players on each team wore the same number. What was it?

Answer Sheet

The Original Six
1 Roll

Name_____

Answer Sheet

The Original Six
1 Roll

Name_____

Answer Sheet

The Original Six
1 Roll

Name_____

1.	1.	1.
2.	2.	2.
3.	3.	3.
4.	4.	4.
5.	5.	5.
6.	6.	6.
7.	7.	7.
8.	8.	8.
9.	9.	9.
10.	10.	10.

After you have filled out the sheet, fold your column underneath along the dashed line so the next restroom user won't see your answers. *The first player uses the far right column.*

Notes:

Notes:

Notes:

The Original Six

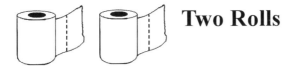

Two Rolls

Flip to pg. 87 for answers

1. This rotund star goaltender for the New York Rangers in the 1950s and 1960s was told by his coach that he had a beer belly. He replied that he didn't drink beer. He only drank scotch. Who was he?

2. What number did Bobby Hull wear when he first joined the Blackhawks? Hint: His son Brett wore it, and it was retired by the St. Louis Blues.

3. Captain of the great Canadiens' teams of the 1960s, he led the NHL in scoring in 1956.

4. Blackhawk Glenn Hall was perhaps the greatest goaltender of the 1960s, but many forget that he started with another team. What team?

5. This legendary coach led the Toronto Maple Leafs to three straight Stanley Cups between 1962-64.

6. This Hall-of-Fame defenseman, who spent 14 years with the Canadiens, became the player-coach of the Rangers in 1961 and led them to the playoffs for the first time in years.

7. In a blockbuster deal on May 15, 1967, the Bruins sent Gilles Marotte, Pit Martin, and Jack Norris to Chicago for Fred Stanfield, Ken Hodge, and one of hockey's all-time leading scorers. Who was he?

8. Throughout the Original Six era, how was it determined who would play whom in the first round of the Stanley Cup Playoffs?

9. Beginning in 1949-50, and ending with expansion in 1967-68, how many games did teams play during the regular season?

10. This brewery owned and sponsored the Montreal Canadiens for many years.

Answer Sheet

The Original Six
2 Rolls

Name_____

1.
2.
3.
4.
5.
6.
7.
8.
9.
10.

Answer Sheet

The Original Six
2 Rolls

Name_____

1.
2.
3.
4.
5.
6.
7.
8.
9.
10.

Answer Sheet

The Original Six
2 Rolls

Name_____

1.
2.
3.
4.
5.
6.
7.
8.
9.
10.

After you have filled out the sheet, fold your column underneath along the dashed line so the next restroom user won't see your answers. *The first player uses the far right column.*

Notes:

Notes:

Notes:

The Original Six

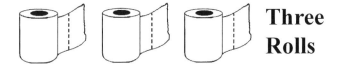

Three Rolls

Flip to pg. 88 for answers

1. When this "seventh team" dropped out after the 1941-42 season, the NHL had its "Original Six" from 1943-1967.

2. Which Original Six team sported black uniforms with many red and white stripes?

3. Known as "The Eel," he probably weighed no more than 150 pounds soaking wet. But this Rangers winger won the Calder Trophy in 1954.

4. He coached the Blackhawks 1961 Stanley Cup championship team.

5. Probably the best player on a bad Bruins team in the early 1960s, he was traded to the Rangers and later became part of a blockbuster deal that sent him and Andy Bathgate to Toronto.

6. Each of the six NHL teams sponsored junior teams which served as their talent pipeline. What team belonged to the Toronto Maple Leafs?

7. Until they moved to the "New Garden" in 1968, the New York Rangers had a hard time scheduling home games when they made the playoffs. Why?

8. Lester Patrick's sons, Muzz and Lynn, coached rival teams during the Original Six era. Muzz coached the Rangers. Who did Lynn coach?

9. Montreal was the scene of a full-scale riot involving over 10,000 people on March 17, 1955. What caused it?

10. "Leapin' Louie" was a hard-nosed defenseman for the Rangers, before moving on to Montreal. His career ended with a devastating injury that left him paralyzed for several weeks. Who was he?

Answer Sheet

The Original Six
3 Rolls

Name_____

Answer Sheet

The Original Six
3 Rolls

Name_____

Answer Sheet

The Original Six
3 Rolls

Name_____

1.	1.	1.
2.	2.	2.
3.	3.	3.
4.	4.	4.
5.	5.	5.
6.	6.	6.
7.	7.	7.
8.	8.	8.
9.	9.	9.
10.	10.	10.

After you have filled out the sheet, fold your column underneath along the dashed line so the next restroom user won't see your answers. ***The first player uses the far right column.***

Notes: *Notes:*   *Notes:*

By the Numbers

One Roll

Flip to pg. 89 for answers

These are all retired or honored uniform numbers. In the event a number is shared, you may identify only one player to be correct.

1. Boston Bruins #4

2. Detroit Red Wings #9

3. Philadelphia Flyers #16

4. New York Islanders #22

5. Pittsburgh Penguins #66

6. Montreal Canadiens #9

7. Boston Bruins #77

8. Montreal Canadiens #4

9. Toronto Maple Leafs #27

10. Calgary Flames #9

Answer Sheet

By the Numbers
1 Roll

Name_____

1.	
2.	
3.	
4.	
5.	
6.	
7.	
8.	
9.	
10.	

Answer Sheet

By the Numbers
1 Roll

Name_____

1.	
2.	
3.	
4.	
5.	
6.	
7.	
8.	
9.	
10.	

Answer Sheet

By the Numbers
1 Roll

Name_____

1.	
2.	
3.	
4.	
5.	
6.	
7.	
8.	
9.	
10.	

After you have filled out the sheet, fold your column underneath along the dashed line so the next restroom user won't see your answers. ***The first player uses the far right column.***

Notes:

Notes:

Notes:

By the Numbers

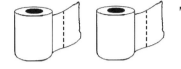

Two Rolls

Flip to pg. 90 for answers

These are all retired or honored uniform numbers. In the event a number is shared, you may identify only one player to be correct.

1. New York Rangers #1

2. Edmonton Oilers #7

3. Buffalo Sabres #11

4. Colorado Avalanche #19

5. Chicago Blackhawks #21

6. New York Islanders #19

7. Detroit Red Wings #19

8. Edmonton Oilers #31

9. Los Angeles Kings #16

10. New York Rangers #7

Answer Sheet

By the Numbers
2 Rolls

Name_____

Answer Sheet

By the Numbers
2 Rolls

Name_____

Answer Sheet

By the Numbers
2 Rolls

Name_____

1.	1.	1.
2.	2.	2.
3.	3.	3.
4.	4.	4.
5.	5.	5.
6.	6.	6.
7.	7.	7.
8.	8.	8.
9.	9.	9.
10.	10.	10.

After you have filled out the sheet, fold your column underneath along the dashed line so the next restroom user won't see your answers. ***The first player uses the far right column.***

Notes:

Notes:

Notes:

By the Numbers

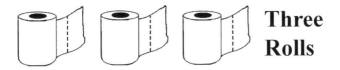

Three Rolls

Flip to pg. 91 for answers

These are all retired or honored uniform numbers. In the event a number is shared, you may identify only one player to be correct.

1. New Jersey Devils #4

2. Toronto Maple Leafs #7

3. Phoenix Coyotes #97

4. Los Angeles Kings #30

5. Colorado Avalanche #21

6. Carolina Hurricanes #10

7. Chicago Blackhawks #35

8. Montreal Canadiens #19

9. Washington Capitals #11

10. Detroit Red Wings #1

Answer Sheet | Answer Sheet | Answer Sheet

By the Numbers
3 Rolls

By the Numbers
3 Rolls

By the Numbers
3 Rolls

Name_____ | Name_____ | Name_____

1.	1.	1.
2.	2.	2.
3.	3.	3.
4.	4.	4.
5.	5.	5.
6.	6.	6.
7.	7.	7.
8.	8.	8.
9.	9.	9.
10.	10.	10.

After you have filled out the sheet, fold your column underneath along the dashed line so the next restroom user won't see your answers. ***The first player uses the far right column.***

Notes: | *Notes:* | *Notes:*

International Hockey

 ## One Roll

Flip to pg. 92 for answers

1. Who was the coach for the US Olympic team's *Miracle on Ice* victory in 1980?

2. Who was the first Russian-trained player to win the Hart Memorial Trophy as the league's MVP? He did it in 1994.

3. What is the name of the high-powered eastern European league which features Dynamo Moscow, Lev Praha (Prague), and Slovan Bratislava?

4. How did Olympic hockey team rosters change beginning in 1998, thereby making Olympic hockey a true world's championship?

5. He was the only Lithuanian in his league when he debuted with Dynamo Moscow in 1988. Years after getting physical with Mario Lemieux in the 1993 playoffs, he became a mainstay on the Pittsburgh blue line.

6. In the 2010 Olympic gold medal game, what American's game-tying goal with 24 seconds to go sent Canada into a panic?

7. Czech out who holds the record for most points in a career by a European player.

8. What was Pavel Bure's nickname?

9. Who was nicknamed *The Finnish Flash*?

10. This number one draft pick from Russia scored 52 goals in his first NHL season (2005-06).

Answer Sheet | # Answer Sheet | # Answer Sheet

International Hockey
1 Roll

International Hockey
1 Roll

International Hockey
1 Roll

Name_____ Name_____ Name_____

1.	1.	1.
2.	2.	2.
3.	3.	3.
4.	4.	4.
5.	5.	5.
6.	6.	6.
7.	7.	7.
8.	8.	8.
9.	9.	9.
10.	10.	10.

After you have filled out the sheet, fold your column underneath along the dashed line so the next restroom user won't see your answers. ***The first player uses the far right column.***

Notes: *Notes:*   *Notes:*

International Hockey

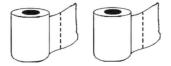

Two Rolls

Flip to pg. 93 for answers

1. After leading Sweden to the Olympic gold medal in 1994, this netminder played 10 NHL seasons with the Islanders, Oilers, and Avalanche.

2. What team did Soviet stars such as Vladislav Tretiak and Valery Kharlamov play for in their homeland?

3. He is Russian, not German. But this goalie is known as *The Bulin Wall*.

4. In 1994, this future NHL superstar's one-handed backhand in a shootout gave Sweden its first Olympic gold medal. Who is he?

5. Who was the US goaltender for the *Miracle on Ice* hockey team in 1980?

6. This future captain of the Ottawa Senators won the Calder Trophy as the league's best rookie in 1996. Name him.

7. Drafted first overall out of Spartak Moscow in 2001, he played several years for the Atlanta Thrashers before being dealt to the New Jersey Devils in February of 2010.

8. Women's hockey became an Olympic sport at the 1998 Games at Nagano, Japan. What country took the gold medal?

9. How did Paul Henderson become a Canadian National Hero?

10. In 1973, the Maple Leafs imported two Swedes, left winger Inge Hammarstrom, and a future Hall of Fame defenseman. Name him.

Answer Sheet | # Answer Sheet | # Answer Sheet

International Hockey 2 Rolls	International Hockey 2 Rolls	International Hockey 2 Rolls

Name_____ Name_____ Name_____

1.	1.	1.
2.	2.	2.
3.	3.	3.
4.	4.	4.
5.	5.	5.
6.	6.	6.
7.	7.	7.
8.	8.	8.
9.	9.	9.
10.	10.	10.

After you have filled out the sheet, fold your column underneath along the dashed line so the next restroom user won't see your answers. *The first player uses the far right column.*

Notes: | *Notes:* | *Notes:*

International Hockey

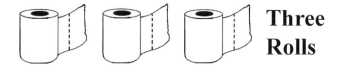

Three Rolls

Flip to pg. 94 for answers

1. Early Swedish import Ulf Sterner played four games for an Original Six team in 1964-65. Which team did he play for?

2. Who was the first Finnish-trained player to play in the NHL?

3. One of the few native Latvians to play in North America, this defenseman debuted for his hometown Dinamo Riga team as a teenager in 1990. He went on to play 15 seasons in the NHL, many of which for the Sharks and Avalanche.

4. In 1977, the Islanders imported their first two Europeans from Sweden. They both played on all four of the Isles' Stanley Cup teams from 1980-1983. Name one of these players.

5. In the 1998 Olympics, Dominik Hasek carried the Czech team to the gold. But what Montreal draft pick/Flyers defenseman scored the only goal in the gold medal game against Russia?

6. On March 13, 1948, who became the first player of Asian descent to ever play in an NHL game? He did so for the New York Rangers.

7. What country boasts the Elitserien, or SEL?

8. Who was the first native-born Russian player permitted by the USSR to join an NHL team? He became a member of the Flames.

9. What country has ELH, or Extraliga ledního hokeje?

10. What former Soviet goalie, argued to be one of the best of all-time, led the Soviet Union to Olympic gold in 1972 and 1976? A few college kids prevented him from winning in 1980.

Answer Sheet

International Hockey
3 Rolls

Name_____

Answer Sheet

International Hockey
3 Rolls

Name_____

Answer Sheet

International Hockey
3 Rolls

Name_____

1.	1.	1.
2.	2.	2.
3.	3.	3.
4.	4.	4.
5.	5.	5.
6.	6.	6.
7.	7.	7.
8.	8.	8.
9.	9.	9.
10.	10.	10.

After you have filled out the sheet, fold your column underneath along the dashed line so the next restroom user won't see your answers. *The first player uses the far right column.*

Notes:

Notes:

Notes:

Everything & Anything

 ## One Roll

Flip to pg. 95 for answers

1. Who generally leads the team onto the ice?

2. Brothers Jack and Steve Carlson had brief NHL careers. But they became much more famous as siblings in a Paul Newman movie. Whom did they portray?

3. What is the name of the vehicle that resurfaces the ice between periods?

4. What phrase, which has been said by just about every hockey announcer, did legendary Toronto broadcaster Foster Hewitt coin?

5. Pittsburgh actually had an NHL team in the mid-late 1920s. What was their name? It really wasn't very unique, having been utilized elsewhere in the city.

6. What were the Carolina Hurricanes known as from 1979-1997?

7. For many years, whose huge portrait hung from the rafters at Maple Leaf Gardens?

8. "Stick save and a beauty" was among the repertoire of this famous American play-by-play man. He would say more than "yes" for a goal.

9. What ocean creature has been often thrown onto the ice by Detroit Red Wings fans?

10. What is the oldest arena in the NHL?

Answer Sheet

Everything & Anything
1 Roll

Name_____

Answer Sheet

Everything & Anything
1 Roll

Name_____

Answer Sheet

Everything & Anything
1 Roll

Name_____

1.	1.	1.
2.	2.	2.
3.	3.	3.
4.	4.	4.
5.	5.	5.
6.	6.	6.
7.	7.	7.
8.	8.	8.
9.	9.	9.
10.	10.	10.

After you have filled out the sheet, fold your column underneath along the dashed line so the next restroom user won't see your answers. *The first player uses the far right column.*

Notes: *Notes:*   *Notes:*

Everything & Anything

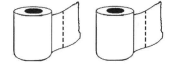

Two Rolls

Flip to pg. 96 for answers

1. This English-speaking play-by-play man for the Montreal Canadiens was famous for colorful phrases such as "a cannonading drive," and "a scintillating save." Name him.

2. What was the nickname of the old Pittsburgh Civic Arena?

3. What does the "CH" stand for on Montreal Canadiens uniforms?

4. This famous bygone arena sat atop North Station.

5. Kansas City's NHL team lasted only two years, playing in 1974-75 and 1975-76. What was their name?

6. Between 1974-1993, the NHL had four divisions named after league builders. Name three of them.

7. Name the arena where the Detroit Red Wings (and forerunners) played from 1927-80.

8. In existence since the 1930s, this league is considered to be hockey's top minor league.

9. What made the ice surface at the Montreal Forum different from other rinks in the 1950s and 1960s?

10. Arenas and St. Patricks were two former names of this long-time NHL team.

Answer Sheet

Everything & Anything
2 Rolls

Name_____

Answer Sheet

Everything & Anything
2 Rolls

Name_____

Answer Sheet

Everything & Anything
2 Rolls

Name_____

1.	1.	1.
2.	2.	2.
3.	3.	3.
4.	4.	4.
5.	5.	5.
6.	6.	6.
7.	7.	7.
8.	8.	8.
9.	9.	9.
10.	10.	10.

After you have filled out the sheet, fold your column underneath along the dashed line so the next restroom user won't see your answers. *The first player uses the far right column.*

Notes:

Notes:

Notes:

Everything & Anything

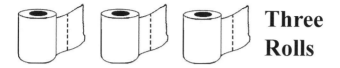

Three Rolls

Flip to pg. 97 for answers

1. What is the name of the mid-winter college hockey tournament held in Boston every year since 1952?

2. Who was the only female goalie to appear in an NHL exhibition game? She did so in 1992 for the Tampa Bay Lightning.

3. Why are the New York Rangers called the Rangers?

4. Chicago Stadium organist Al Melgard incurred the wrath of NHL management for something he would play as the officials entered the ice. What did he play?

5. When the roof of Philadelphia's Spectrum blew off in 1968, in what Canadian city did the Flyers play five of their remaining home games?

6. On December 6, 2011, Hurricanes goalie Mike Murphy made his NHL debut. He took the loss without ever letting up a goal! How on earth did this happen?

7. Baseball's Charlie Finley briefly owned the California Golden Seals. How were his players' skates truly unique?

8. In the 1940s, Fern Gauthier of the Detroit Red Wings went down to a New York pier, hockey stick in hand. What was he trying to prove?

9. Although better known as the organist for the Brooklyn Dodgers at Ebbets Field, she actually started earlier at Madison Square Garden. She was the answer to the trick question, "Who is the only person to play for the Dodgers, Knicks, and Rangers?"

10. This arena housed the famous 3,663-pipe Barton organ, one of the largest pipe organs in the US.

Answer Sheet

Everything & Anything
3 Rolls

Name_____

Answer Sheet

Everything & Anything
3 Rolls

Name_____

Answer Sheet

Everything & Anything
3 Rolls

Name_____

1.	1.	1.
2.	2.	2.
3.	3.	3.
4.	4.	4.
5.	5.	5.
6.	6.	6.
7.	7.	7.
8.	8.	8.
9.	9.	9.
10.	10.	10.

After you have filled out the sheet, fold your column underneath along the dashed line so the next restroom user won't see your answers. *The first player uses the far right column.*

Notes: *Notes:*   *Notes:*

Greatest Moments

 ## One Roll — Answers

1. The US Olympic hockey team's improbable 4-3 victory over the Soviet Union

2. Sidney Crosby

3. Bobby Hull

4. Patrick Kane. It was a confusing scene, as most of the fans, and even the announcers, were unsure if the puck crossed the goal line. It did, and Kane used the entire rink to celebrate.

5. Mario Lemieux

6. Wayne Gretzky

7. Bob Nystrom. At 7:11 of overtime against Philadelphia. It was the third Cup won on an OT goal in eleven seasons. In 1977, Jacques Lemaire was the hero for Montreal. In 1970, Bruins legend Bobby Orr famously flew through the air as the puck crossed the goal line.

8. Patrick Roy

9. He put on a goalie mask. After a shot from Rangers' Andy Bathgate broke his nose, he returned to the ice wearing a mask.

10. Edmonton. Though Gretzky was a member of the Kings at the time, most of his 1,851 points were accumulated as an Oiler.

Greatest Moments

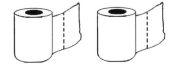 ## Two Rolls — Answers

1. Maurice Richard. He suffered a concussion and never remembered the game. Of course today, he would not have been allowed back onto the ice.

2. He notched 6 goals and 4 assists for 10 points in a game against the Boston Bruins

3. Derek Stepan

4. Willie O'Ree of the Boston Bruins

5. The US won the Olympic gold medal in hockey for the first time

6. Bobby Carpenter of the Washington Capitals

7. Stephane Matteau's double-OT goal in Game 7 of the 1994 Eastern Conference Finals lifted the Rangers to a 2-1 victory over the Devils. The Rangers went on to win their first Stanley Cup since 1940.

8. Pat LaFontaine. Unrelated, but interesting, is that later that night *The Simpsons* aired for the first time as a cartoon-short on the *Tracey Ullman Show*.

9. Canada lost the first game of the Summit Series to the Soviet Union, 7-3. They were expected to dominate the Soviets. Canada eventually won the series.

10. The first NHL All-Star Game. It was staged as a benefit to aid injured Maple Leaf Ace Bailey. The Maple Leafs defeated a team of All-Stars, 7-3. Regular All-Star Games began in 1947.

Greetest Moments

Three Rolls —
Answers

1. He ended the longest game in playoff history with a goal at 16:30 of the 6th overtime to beat the Montreal Maroons, 1-0

2. Bill Barilko

3. He set an NHL record for shorthanded goals in a game with 3

4. Most goals in one game - 7

5. He scored three goals in 21 seconds against the New York Rangers

6. Gordon (Red) Berenson for the St. Louis Blues at Philadelphia

7. They scored 16 goals on the road against the Quebec Bulldogs

8. They were shut out for the eighth consecutive game

9. Ian Turnbull

10. Pete Babando. The Red Wings defeated the Rangers.

Wings & Centers

One Roll — Answers

1. Bobby Hull. His son would become the "Golden Brett."

2. Mike Bossy

3. Dave "The Hammer" Schultz

4. Phil Esposito of the Boston Bruins

5. Marcel Dionne

6. Oilers, Kings, Blues, Rangers. He also played for the Indianapolis Racers and Edmonton Oilers in the WHA.

7. Jaromir Jagr

8. Mike Modano - 561. He also leads all American-born players in points with 1,374.

9. Lanny McDonald

10. Evgeni Malkin

Wings & Centers

 ## Two Rolls — Answers

1. Joe Mullen. He was the first American to score 500 goals.

2. Clark Gillies

3. Most career penalty minutes - 3,966

4. Frank Mahovlich

5. Ron Francis

6. Luc Robitaille - 668

7. Yvan Cournoyer

8. Adam Oates

9. Teemu Selänne

10. Brett Hull

Wings & Centers

Three Rolls — Answers

1. Houston Aeros and the New England Whalers. The New England Whalers became the Hartford Whalers of the NHL. Howe played in their inaugural season of 1979-80, and netted 15 goals. He was 52 years-old by the end of the season.

2. Howie Morenz. On January 28, 1937, he broke his leg in a game against Chicago. His health failed while he was hospitalized, and he died about six weeks later.

3. Vic Hadfield, Jean Ratelle, Rod Gilbert

4. André Lacroix with 251 goals, 547 assists, and 798 points

5. Dale Hawerchuk with 929 points in a Jets uniform. He finished with 1,409 points in his career.

6. The Production Line

7. Bill Masterton. The Bill Masterton Memorial Trophy is awarded to a player for his dedication, sportsmanship, and perseverance.

8. Brian Lawton. He finished his career with 266 points.

9. Doug Jarvis with 964 (1975-1987)

10. The Kraut Line. Anti-German sentiment during the early years of WWII necessitated a change in the line's name to the Kitchener Kids.

Between the Pipes

 ## One Roll — Answers

1. John Vanbiesbrouck

2. Henrik Lundqvist

3. Patrick Roy. His 551 wins were surpassed by Martin Brodeur in 2009. The draft fittingly took place at the Montreal Forum.

4. Georges Vezina was the Canadiens' goalie from 1910 to 1925. He collapsed in the crease from tuberculosis on November 28, 1925, and died March 27, 1926.

5. Ron Hextall. 584 minutes in 608 games.

6. Roberto Luongo

7. Ken Dryden

8. Curtis Joseph. His nickname was "Cujo."

9. Bill Smith in 1981-82

10. Dominik Hasek

Between the Pipes

 ## Two Rolls — Answers

1. He played in 502 consecutive games. The streak started in 1955 and ended in 1962.

2. Bill Smith of the Islanders in 1979. On a delayed penalty, a pass from Rob Ramage of the Colorado Rockies missed its mark and traveled the length of the ice into an open net. Smith was the last Islander to touch it. Ron Hextall was the first to score on an actual shot… and he did it twice.

3. 83 shots. He made 80 saves as the Blackhawks lost to the Bruins 3-2.

4. Arturs Irbe

5. "Inski." He finished his short career with a 2-6-1 record, and a GAA just shy of 6.

6. Rinks had a spare goaltender on hand. Often they were off-ice officials (formerly called minor officials).

7. Chris Osgood went 14-4 with a 1.55 GAA in the 2008 Playoffs

8. Miikka Kiprusoff. Brian Elliott of the Blues eclipsed this mark with a 1.56 GAA in 2011-2012. It should be noted that Kiprusoff and Elliott both played in only 38 games.

9. Tony Esposito of the Chicago Blackhawks

10. Gerry Cheevers of the Boston Bruins

Between the Pipes

 **Three Rolls — Answers**

1. Johnny Bower

2. Clint Malarchuk. The ice was flooded with blood shortly thereafter. Trainer, and former army medic, Jim Pizzutelli saved his life.

3. Jack McCartan. He later played for the Minnesota Fighting Saints of the WHA.

4. Frank Brimsek

5. Rick DiPietro (2000, Islanders) and Marc-Andre Fleury (2003, Penguins)

6. Gilles Gilbert won 17 straight games in 1975-76

7. Ed Giacomin and Gilles Villemure. In those days, the trophy was awarded to the goalie(s) of the team who had given up the fewest goals.

8. A baseball first baseman's mitt…with a little additional leather going up the sleeve

9. Most losses by a goaltender in a season. He lost 48 games in 1970-71.

10. Terry Sawchuk

Stanley Cup Playoffs

 ## One Roll — Answers

1. Montreal Canadiens - 24

2. A labor dispute cancelled the entire 2004-05 season

3. Martin Brodeur and Patrick Roy. On April 19, 2012, Brodeur took over the top spot with his 24th playoff shutout.

4. Henri Richard played on 11 Cup winners, all with the Montreal Canadiens

5. Philadelphia Flyers in 1974. They also won the following year.

6. Lord Stanley

7. Nine seconds. Brian Skrudland's goal at 0:09 lifted the Montreal Canadiens to a 3-2 victory over the Calgary Flames in Game 2 of the 1986 Stanley Cup Finals. Montreal won the series 4 games to 1. In the first round of the 1975 playoffs, it took Islander J.P. Parise only 11 seconds to light the lamp to eliminate the Rangers. In the 2011 Finals, Vancouver's Alex Burrows buried an OT goal against the Bruins after just 11 seconds as well.

8. Wayne Gretzky - 122 for Edmonton, Los Angeles, St. Louis, and the New York Rangers

9. Scotty Bowman - 9. He won five times with the Montreal Canadiens, once with the Pittsburgh Penguins, and three more times with the Detroit Red Wings.

10. Overtime goals in the Stanley Cup playoffs

Stanley Cup Playoffs

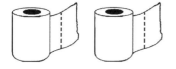 **Two Rolls — Answers**

1. Montreal goaltender Ken Dryden won the Conn Smythe Trophy in 1971, and then the Calder in 1972

2. The 1942 Maple Leafs beat the Red Wings in the Stanley Cup Finals. The 1975 Islanders beat the Penguins in the quarterfinals. The 2010 Flyers beat the Bruins in the Eastern Conference Semifinals.

3. Dale Hunter

4. Chris Chelios made the playoffs 24 times with Montreal, Chicago, and Detroit. Coincidentally, much of his career he wore number 24.

5. Boston Bruins, 1968-96

6. It sits permanently in the Hall of Fame in Toronto. After concerns were raised about the condition of the original Cup, a new *Presentation Cup* was created.

7. Dallas Stars - 1999; Tampa Bay Lightning - 2004; Carolina Hurricanes - 2006

8. Jacques Lemaire. He won the eight Stanley Cups playing for the Canadiens, and then coached the New Jersey Devils to the title.

9. Detroit Red Wings - 11

10. He was the majority owner of the Toronto Maple Leafs from 1927-1961 and the builder of Maple Leaf Gardens

Stanley Cup Playoffs

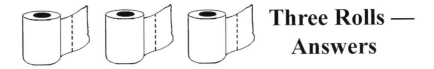

Three Rolls — Answers

1. David Volek

2. Seattle Metropolitans

3. Bob Baun

4. Bill Stewart. Born in Massachusetts, he not only coached the Black-hawks, but was also a National League umpire for 21 years.

5. Some years, the Cup was awarded to the team that scored the most goals during the course of the series

6. Derian Hatcher - Dallas Stars, 1999; Dustin Brown - LA Kings, 2012

7. Fourteen. Needless to say, the game was a little different back then.

8. The Montreal Amateur Athletic Association won the first Stanley Cup back in 1893. The Cup was inscribed as the "Dominion Hockey Challenge Cup."

9. The finals were called off after five games because of the global flu epidemic. Montreal Canandien defenseman Bad Joe Hall died of the disease.

10. New York Islanders - 19 series from 1980-84

Defensemen

 ## One Roll — Answers

1. Ray Bourque

2. Denis Potvin

3. They had a low, single digit number. Not all, but most defensemen had numbers between 2 and 6.

4. Scott Niedermayer

5. Chris Chelios

6. Bryan Leetch of the Rangers in 1994. Goalies Tim Thomas (2011) and Jonathan Quick (2012) are the only other Americans to win the Conn Smythe.

7. P. K. Subban in 2011

8. Detroit's Nicklas Lidstrom in 2001. He won a total of seven of them.

9. Erik Karlsson

10. Paul Coffey for the 1985-86 Oilers

Defensemen

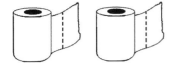 ## Two Rolls — Answers

1. Ken Daneyko

2. Ken Morrow. First he won a gold medal with the US *Miracle on Ice* team, and then he hoisted the Stanley Cup with the New York Islanders.

3. Ed Jovanovski

4. Doug Harvey. He won seven of the first nine Norris Trophies.

5. Eddie Shore

6. Brad Park

7. Kevin Hatcher. He scored 34 in 1992-93.

8. Rob Blake in 1998

9. Al Arbour

10. Chris Pronger

Defensemen

Three Rolls —
Answers

1. Reijo Ruotsalainen

2. Leonard "Red" Kelly

3. Larry Zeidel

4. Rod Langway

5. Randy Carlyle

6. Jacques Laperriere

7. Steve Smith. In attempting to clear the zone, the puck clipped the back of Grant Fuhr's leg and trickled into the net. Calgary's Perry Berezan was credited with the goal. The mistake occurred on Smith's 23rd birthday.

8. Harry Howell

9. Bryan Berard

10. Pierre Pilote

Rules & Refs

 ## One Roll — Answers

1. 6 feet wide x 4 feet high. The same dimensions as a batter's box in baseball.

2. Five minutes

3. It was a tie game. Each team received one point in the league standings.

4. Delay of game for shooting the puck over the glass. If the puck nips the glass, no penalty is called. This new interpretation, enacted in 2005, has created OT chances in the playoffs. It's hard for a referee to swallow the whistle on this one.

5. Offside

6. The goal judge

7. Three inches. And it's one inch thick.

8. Icing

9. The linesmen

10. Twelve inches. The red line is twelve inches wide as well.

Rules & Refs

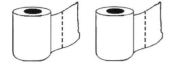

1. Diving

2. Neil Armstrong

3. Orange

4. Using one hand to chop the other forearm

5. It was a rectangle

6. Interference

7. Penalty shot

8. The stick cannot be higher than the crossbar

9. Goaltenders may not play the puck outside the trapezoid area. If they do, it's a 2-minute penalty.

10. It limited the curvature of the blade to 1½ inches. The current maximum is three-quarters of an inch. It was Mikita who "invented" the curved blade—completely by accident. According to Mikita, during a practice session the blade of his stick got stuck in the door to the bench and bent. He didn't want to go all the way back to the dressing room to get another one, so he continued using it. He and his teammates were amazed how the puck dipped when he shot it with the curved blade.

Rules & Refs

Three Rolls — Answers

1. It was based on longevity. The senior referee wore Number 1, and so on.

2. Bill Chadwick

3. It's a goal. Players may legally kick the puck to a teammate. If a player passes the puck with their hand in the offensive zone, it is a "hand-pass," and a face-off results.

4. The rule went into effect in October, 2005 after the lockout

5. Kerry Fraser. He refereed over 2,000 regular season and playoff games.

6. A player serving a minor penalty was allowed to return to the ice if the team on the power play scored a goal. The Canadiens often scored two or more goals during a full two-minute power play.

7. Charging

8. The referee points to center ice

9. It goes back to the early days of black and white television. It was difficult to distinguish which line was which, so the red line was checked. Everything's in color now, but the tradition has remained.

10. Eight feet wide

The Original Six

 ## One Roll — Answers

1. Boston Bruins, Chicago Blackhawks, Detroit Red Wings, Montreal Canadiens, New York Rangers, Toronto Maple Leafs

2. Detroit Red Wings

3. Bobby Orr, for the Boston Bruins against the Detroit Red Wings. He got his first assist.

4. Maurice Richard, and younger brother Henri Richard

5. Emile Francis

6. Saturday

7. Bernie (Boom-Boom) Geoffrion

8. Clarence Campbell

9. Toe Blake

10. Nine. Blackhawks - Bobby Hull, Bruins - Johnny Bucyk, Canadiens - Maurice Richard, Maple Leafs - Dick Duff, Rangers - Andy Bathgate, Red Wings - Gordie Howe.

The Original Six

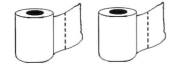 **Two Rolls — Answers**

1. Lorne (Gump) Worsley

2. Sixteen

3. Jean Beliveau

4. Detroit Red Wings

5. Punch Imlach

6. Doug Harvey

7. Phil Esposito

8. The first place team would play the third place team. The second place team would play the fourth place team. The winners would meet for the Stanley Cup.

9. 70 games

10. Molson

The Original Six

 **Three Rolls —
Answers**

1. Brooklyn Americans. But they didn't play in Brooklyn. They played at Madison Square Garden in Manhattan.

2. Chicago Blackhawks

3. Camille Henry

4. Rudy Pilous

5. Don McKenney

6. Toronto Marlboros. They have nearly a century of history behind them.

7. The circus took over Madison Square Garden, and in those days they were unable to put the circus floor over the ice

8. Boston Bruins

9. Maurice Richard had been suspended for the remainder of the season for deliberating hitting a Boston player with his stick in an earlier game. The conflict was called the "Richard Riot."

10. Lou Fontinato

By the Numbers

 ## One Roll — Answers

1. Bobby Orr

2. Gordie Howe

3. Bobby Clarke

4. Mike Bossy

5. Mario Lemieux

6. Maurice Richard

7. Raymond Bourque

8. Jean Beliveau

9. Frank Mahovlich, Darryl Sittler

10. Lanny McDonald

By the Numbers

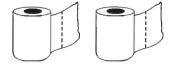 **Two Rolls — Answers**

1. Ed Giacomin

2. Paul Coffey

3. Gilbert Perreault

4. Joe Sakic

5. Stan Mikita

6. Bryan Trottier

7. Steve Yzerman

8. Grant Fuhr

9. Marcel Dionne

10. Rod Gilbert

By the Numbers

Three Rolls — Answers

1. Scott Stevens

2. King Clancy, Tim Horton

3. Jeremy Roenick

4. Rogatien Vachon

5. Peter Forsberg

6. Ron Francis

7. Tony Esposito

8. Larry Robinson

9. Mike Gartner

10. Terry Sawchuk

International Hockey

 ## One Roll — Answers

1. Herb Brooks

2. Sergei Fedorov as a member of the Detroit Red Wings. He scored 56 goals and notched 120 points that season.

3. Kontinental Hockey League (KHL)

4. NHL players were permitted to compete

5. Darius Kasparaitis

6. Zach Parise. In OT, Sidney Crosby's goal allowed the entire country to exhale.

7. Jaromir Jagr

8. *The Russian Rocket*

9. Teemu Selänne

10. Alex Ovechkin

International Hockey

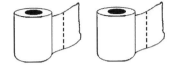 **Two Rolls — Answers**

1. Tommy Salo

2. Red Army (CSKA Moscow)

3. Nikolai Khabibulin

4. Peter Forsberg

5. Jim Craig

6. Sweden's Daniel Alfredsson

7. Ilya Kovalchuk

8. The US defeated Canada in the finals to take home the first gold medal in women's Olympic ice hockey

9. He scored with 34 seconds remaining to lift Canada over the USSR in Game 8 of the 1972 Summit Series. Canada won the series, 4-3, with one tie.

10. Borje Salming

International Hockey

Three Rolls — Answers

1. New York Rangers

2. Matti Hagman for the Bruins in 1976. Pentti Lund, who played seven seasons in the NHL in the late 40s and early 50s, was born in Finland, but grew up in Canada.

3. Sandis Ozolinsh

4. Stefan Persson and Anders Kallur

5. Petr Svoboda

6. Larry Kwong. He played one shift.

7. Sweden has the Swedish Elite League

8. Sergei Priakin debuted in 1989, just in time to get a Stanley Cup ring

9. The Czech Republic

10. Vladislav Tretiak. Coach Viktor Tikhonov pulled him from the *Miracle on Ice* game after he let up a goal in the last second of the 1st period. Tretiak went on to become president of the Ice Hockey Federation of Russia.

Everything & Anything

 ## One Roll — Answers

1. The starting goaltender

2. They were two of the Hanson Brothers in the movie *Slap Shot*. The third brother was played by Dave Hanson, who also played briefly in the NHL.

3. Zamboni

4. "He shoots, he scores!" Hewitt called his first game way back in 1923.

5. Pittsburgh Pirates. They moved to Philadelphia in 1930-31 and lasted one year as the Quakers.

6. Hartford Whalers

7. Queen Elizabeth II

8. Marv Albert

9. An octopus. The tradition began on April 15, 1952, when Pete and Jerry Cusimano threw one onto the ice. The 8 tentacles represented the number of victories the Red Wings needed to win the Cup in those days.

10. New York's Madison Square Garden. The Rangers played their first game there on February 18, 1968. However the arena has been completely modernized.

Everything & Anything

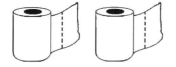

Two Rolls — Answers

1. Danny Gallivan

2. The Igloo

3. Club de Hockey

4. Boston Garden

5. Kansas City Scouts. They became the Colorado Rockies, and finally the New Jersey Devils.

6. Adams, Norris, Patrick, and Smythe

7. Detroit Olympia (or Olympia Stadium). The team became known as the Red Wings in 1932-33. Before that, they were the Cougars and Falcons.

8. American Hockey League (AHL). Its first President was Maurice Podoloff, who later became the first executive of what became the National Basketball Association.

9. The ice was light blue

10. Toronto Maple Leafs

Everything & Anything

 ## Three Rolls — Answers

1. The Beanpot

2. Manon Rhéaume stopped 7 of 9 shots in one period against the Blues

3. "Tex" Rickard was the head of Madison Square Garden at the time. He loved the real Texas Rangers lawmen. So the team became known as Tex's Rangers.

4. He played *Three Blind Mice* when the referee and linesmen skated onto the ice

5. Quebec City, at Le Colisée

6. When starter Cam Ward was pulled after allowing 6 goals to the Flames, Murphy came in and stopped both shots he faced. Trailing 6-4, he was pulled for an extra skater. But, Jarome Iginla scored an empty-netter for the Flames. Murphy returned to the net and in the last minute, the Hurricanes scored twice. They lost 7-6. Being that the 7th goal was scored on his watch, Murphy took the loss…without ever allowing a goal in the NHL. In 2012, Murphy decided to play in Russia.

7. They wore white skates, just as Finley's Oakland A's wore white baseball shoes

8. That he could shoot the puck in the ocean. Gauthier was actually being a good sport in helping out a *Detroit Times* writer. He allowed the scribe to report that he missed his first two shots, the first being snatched by an airborne seagull, and the second landing on a moving barge.

9. Gladys Goodding

10. Chicago Stadium

Scorecard — Name: _____

Category	# Right		# of Pts.		Tot. Pts.
Greatest Moments - 1 Roll		x	1	=	
Greatest Moments - 2 Rolls		x	2	=	
Greatest Moments - 3 Rolls		x	3	=	
Wings & Centers - 1 Roll		x	1	=	
Wings & Centers - 2 Rolls		x	2	=	
Wings & Centers - 3 Rolls		x	3	=	
Between the Pipes - 1 Roll		x	1	=	
Between the Pipes - 2 Rolls		x	2	=	
Between the Pipes - 3 Rolls		x	3	=	
Stanley Cup Playoffs - 1 Roll		x	1	=	
Stanley Cup Playoffs - 2 Rolls		x	2	=	
Stanley Cup Playoffs - 3 Rolls		x	3	=	
Defensemen - 1 Roll		x	1	=	
Defensemen - 2 Rolls		x	2	=	
Defensemen - 3 Rolls		x	3	=	
Rules & Refs - 1 Roll		x	1	=	
Rules & Refs - 2 Rolls		x	2	=	
Rules & Refs - 3 Rolls		x	3	=	
The Original Six - 1 Roll		x	1	=	
The Original Six - 2 Rolls		x	2	=	
The Original Six - 3 Rolls		x	3	=	
By the Numbers - 1 Roll		x	1	=	
By the Numbers - 2 Rolls		x	2	=	
By the Numbers - 3 Rolls		x	3	=	
International Hockey - 1 Roll		x	1	=	
International Hockey - 2 Rolls		x	2	=	
International Hockey - 3 Rolls		x	3	=	
Everything & Anything - 1 Roll		x	1	=	
Everything & Anything - 2 Rolls		x	2	=	
Everything & Anything - 3 Rolls		x	3	=	

Grand Total

Scorecard — Name: _____

Category	# Right		# of Pts.		Tot. Pts.
Greatest Moments - 1 Roll		x	1	=	
Greatest Moments - 2 Rolls		x	2	=	
Greatest Moments - 3 Rolls		x	3	=	
Wings & Centers - 1 Roll		x	1	=	
Wings & Centers - 2 Rolls		x	2	=	
Wings & Centers - 3 Rolls		x	3	=	
Between the Pipes - 1 Roll		x	1	=	
Between the Pipes - 2 Rolls		x	2	=	
Between the Pipes - 3 Rolls		x	3	=	
Stanley Cup Playoffs - 1 Roll		x	1	=	
Stanley Cup Playoffs - 2 Rolls		x	2	=	
Stanley Cup Playoffs - 3 Rolls		x	3	=	
Defensemen - 1 Roll		x	1	=	
Defensemen - 2 Rolls		x	2	=	
Defensemen - 3 Rolls		x	3	=	
Rules & Refs - 1 Roll		x	1	=	
Rules & Refs - 2 Rolls		x	2	=	
Rules & Refs - 3 Rolls		x	3	=	
The Original Six - 1 Roll		x	1	=	
The Original Six - 2 Rolls		x	2	=	
The Original Six - 3 Rolls		x	3	=	
By the Numbers - 1 Roll		x	1	=	
By the Numbers - 2 Rolls		x	2	=	
By the Numbers - 3 Rolls		x	3	=	
International Hockey - 1 Roll		x	1	=	
International Hockey - 2 Rolls		x	2	=	
International Hockey - 3 Rolls		x	3	=	
Everything & Anything - 1 Roll		x	1	=	
Everything & Anything - 2 Rolls		x	2	=	
Everything & Anything - 3 Rolls		x	3	=	

Grand Total

Scorecard — Name: _____

Category	# Right		# of Pts.		Tot. Pts.
Greatest Moments - 1 Roll		x	1	=	
Greatest Moments - 2 Rolls		x	2	=	
Greatest Moments - 3 Rolls		x	3	=	
Wings & Centers - 1 Roll		x	1	=	
Wings & Centers - 2 Rolls		x	2	=	
Wings & Centers - 3 Rolls		x	3	=	
Between the Pipes - 1 Roll		x	1	=	
Between the Pipes - 2 Rolls		x	2	=	
Between the Pipes - 3 Rolls		x	3	=	
Stanley Cup Playoffs - 1 Roll		x	1	=	
Stanley Cup Playoffs - 2 Rolls		x	2	=	
Stanley Cup Playoffs - 3 Rolls		x	3	=	
Defensemen - 1 Roll		x	1	=	
Defensemen - 2 Rolls		x	2	=	
Defensemen - 3 Rolls		x	3	=	
Rules & Refs - 1 Roll		x	1	=	
Rules & Refs - 2 Rolls		x	2	=	
Rules & Refs - 3 Rolls		x	3	=	
The Original Six - 1 Roll		x	1	=	
The Original Six - 2 Rolls		x	2	=	
The Original Six - 3 Rolls		x	3	=	
By the Numbers - 1 Roll		x	1	=	
By the Numbers - 2 Rolls		x	2	=	
By the Numbers - 3 Rolls		x	3	=	
International Hockey - 1 Roll		x	1	=	
International Hockey - 2 Rolls		x	2	=	
International Hockey - 3 Rolls		x	3	=	
Everything & Anything - 1 Roll		x	1	=	
Everything & Anything - 2 Rolls		x	2	=	
Everything & Anything - 3 Rolls		x	3	=	

Grand Total

How did you do?

500 +   — King/Queen of the Throne

400-499 — Topper of the Hopper

350-399 — Porcelain Prince/Princess

300-349 — Toileterrific!

250-299 — Keep Flushing for the Stars

200-249 — Might Need a Plunger

150-199 — Gotta call the Plumber

Below 150 — Clogged

Try a different Toiletrivia Book!

37601164R00058

Made in the USA
San Bernardino, CA
01 June 2019